Manners for the Metropolis: An Entrance Key to the Fantastic Life of the 400

Frank Crowninshield

Nabu Public Domain Reprints:

You are holding a reproduction of an original work published before 1923 that is in the public domain in the United States of America, and possibly other countries. You may freely copy and distribute this work as no entity (individual or corporate) has a copyright on the body of the work. This book may contain prior copyright references, and library stamps (as most of these works were scanned from library copies). These have been scanned and retained as part of the historical artifact.

This book may have occasional imperfections such as missing or blurred pages, poor pictures, errant marks, etc. that were either part of the original artifact, or were introduced by the scanning process. We believe this work is culturally important, and despite the imperfections, have elected to bring it back into print as part of our continuing commitment to the preservation of printed works worldwide. We appreciate your understanding of the imperfections in the preservation process, and hope you enjoy this valuable book.

MANNERS
for the
METROPOLIS

MANNERS
for the
METROPOLIS

*An Entrance Key to the
Fantastic Life of
The 400*

BY

FRANCIS W. CROWNINSHIELD

DECORATIONS BY
LOUIS FANCHER

NEW YORK
D. APPLETON AND COMPANY
1908

COPYRIGHT, 1908, BY
D. APPLETON AND COMPANY

COPYRIGHT, 1908, BY
THE METROPOLITAN MAGAZINE COMPANY

Published, October, 1908

TO

H. S. C.

CONTENTS

	PAGE
FOREWORD	3
COUNTRY HOUSES	9
CONVERSATION	27
DINNERS	35
DANCES	53
BRIDGE	65
THE THEATER	85
CALLING	91
OUR COUNTRY COUSINS	95
NEWPORT	103
GENERAL RULES	113

LIST OF ILLUSTRATIONS

	FACING PAGE
TIPS . . . . *Frontispiece*	
CONVERSATION	28
HOSTESS	60
BRIDGE	78

FOREWORD

IT is undeniable that much of the pleasure in modern life is derived from social intercourse.

From time immemorial the gregarious instinct has contributed greatly to the charm of all populated regions. It is worthy of remark that, during the past decade, both in America and in England, sudden and violent changes have somewhat ruffled the placid waters of polite society. These new conditions of life have naturally necessitated new methods of social procedure. The telephone, coeducation, wireless telegraphy, motor cars, millionaires, bridge whist, women's rights, Sherry's, cocktails, four-day liners, pianolas, steam heat, *directoire* gowns, dirigible balloons, and talking machines have all contributed to an astonishing social metamorphosis.

Curiously enough no book of etiquette has taken count of these violent changes. There is literally no Baedeker for this newly discovered country. Many fruitful and enchanted islands have been sighted, but have, alas, remained uncharted.

It is, therefore, with motives of generosity, charity, and kindness that this little guide has been prepared by the benevolent author.

It will be found to contain concise rules of deportment for all the more important social ceremonies—from a *tête-à-tête* to a betrothal, a picnic to a funeral, a *partie-carrée* to a divorce, an ushers' dinner to a Turkish bath, and a piano recital to a rout. It also contains excellent advice on the choice of a motor car, a summer residence, a wife, or a brand of cigar.

The author feels that it should prove of great value to those people who have been born and brought up in refined and well-bred families, and are, at the same time, desirous of entering fashionable society.

To our newer millionaires and plutocrats it should be a very present help in time of trouble, for it is undeniable that many of these captains of industry—however strong and virile their natures—become utterly helpless and panic-stricken at the mere sight of a gold finger bowl, an alabaster bath, a pronged oyster fork, or the business end of an asparagus.

COUNTRY HOUSES

A COUNTRY HOUSE is an establishment maintained by people of wealth and position who have banished from their home circle the old ideas of family life: the hearthside, the romping little ones, and the studious evenings under the red lamp.

※

THERE is so much that is pleasurable in a house party at such an establishment that it is difficult to say which part of it is the most delightful. It is thrilling to receive the invitation; the journey there is full of an expectant pleasure; the sport is invigorating; the meals are usually palatable; the society agreeable. On the whole, however, perhaps the most welcome part of it all is the moment of departure.

※

At a week-end party, when the servant calls you in the morning and informs you that your bath is running, it is modish to sink off to sleep and allow the bath to overflow. As soon as you are wide awake make certain to turn off the electric light and demand from the servant a brandy and soda. After this bracer you may light a cigarette and send the footman for breakfast and a cigar. It is also a wise precaution to ask for *all* the morning papers—otherwise the other guests may secure some of them.

※

It is usual for the bachelors to dawdle about in their riding things until lunch is announced. They can then go to their rooms, take their baths, and change. This puts off the agony of the lunch—which is always a tiresome meal.

※

Go up early to dress for dinner, or the other guests will have drawn off all the hot water for their own baths.

※

After a week-end visit it is customary to write your hostess a "bread-and-butter letter," or "pleaser." The following note will be found a safe guide for such an occasion.

My dear Mrs. Weekende:

How kind you were to open the gates of Heaven and give me that little glimpse of Paradise. Would you be good enough to ask the valet to send me my cap? Perhaps, too, the footman could forward my golf clubs, which I

MANNERS *for the* METROPOLIS

entirely overlooked in the hurry of departure. If not too much trouble, perhaps you will ask the maid to express me my sponge bag, listerine, and razor strop.

With renewed thanks, I am, dear Mrs. Weekende,
   Yours sincerely,
    PERCY VANDERFORT.

P. S.—I am returning to you, by express, the woodland violet bath salt, the photograph frame, the bedroom clock, the silver brushes, the hot-water bag, and the two sachet cases which your servant mistook for my property.

WHEN you are visiting in the country and your hostess maintains a very small establishment, the servant may ask you, on awaking you, what you desire for breakfast.

Out of consideration for your hostess you should ask for a very small and very simple breakfast. Try to confine yourself to grape fruit, oatmeal, bacon and eggs, corn bread, chicken mince, marmalade, coffee, honey, hot biscuits, and orange juice.

Parlor tricks are great assets in a week-ender. The most popular are moving the scalp and ears, cracking the knuckles, disjointing the thumbs, standing on the head, tearing a pack of cards, and dancing a cake walk.

When the host offers, after breakfast, to show you over the farm, gasp, and mention your rheumatism. Almost any lie is permissible to prevent so terrible a catastrophe.

Young girls, when visiting at a house party, should be quiet and gentle, well behaved and agreeable; but when at home there is no reason why they should not be perfectly natural.

The horrors of the guest room are too well known to need enumeration, and can seldom be ameliorated. They are, roughly, as follows: The embroidered pillow slips, the egg-finished sheets, the drawer of the bureau that is warped and will not open, the rusty pins in the stony pincushion, the empty cut-glass cologne bottles, the blinds that bang in the night, the absence of hooks on which to hang your razor strop, the pictures of the "Huguenot Lovers" and Landseer's "Sanctuary" over the headboard of the bed, the tendency of the maid to hide the matches, the dear little children in the nursery above

MANNERS for the METROPOLIS

you, the dead fly in the dried-up ink well, and the hidden radiator under the sofa.

※

WHEN you spend Sunday in the country, the proper schedule of tips for the servants is as follows:

Chauffeur	$10.00
Butler	10.00
Coachman	5.00
Footman	3.00
Valet	5.00
Cook	nothing
Maid	2.00
Chambermaid	2.00
Strapper	1.00
Groom	2.00
Total	$40.00

Should you, however, have but $30 with you, you have but to take a very early train, in which case the butler will not have appeared, and there will be no necessity to tip him. The resourceful bachelor may also decide to compensate the maid, if she be pretty, by a few pleasant words of appreciation as to her beauty and by chucking her under the chin, as is invariably done on the stage in comic opera.

If your visit has been for a week, the above table of tips should be disregarded. At the end of such a visit you had best hand the housekeeper a letter of introduction to your lawyer, together with a list of your securities, and allow her to sue your estate for the gratuities.

(If you are from Pittsburg, care should be taken to double the above table of tips.)

THE dressing gong is sometimes meant to convey the impression that dinner will shortly be served in the banqueting hall. Usually, however, it is the signal for everybody to begin a new rubber.

TRY to go early to the stables and select a good riding horse for the rest of your visit. There are seldom more than two good ones. The rest are usually roarers or crocks.

THE hostess at a large country house is naturally expected to provide all the week-end essentials—i. e., liquors, cigars, food, carriages—and motors in condition. Besides these, however, she should never neglect to offer her guests certain little added comforts without which they would, very naturally, be miserable. Every guest should be supplied, therefore, with the following articles: a bottle of listerine, a cloth cap, a tennis bat, a

MANNERS *for the* METROPOLIS

hot-water bag, a pair of motor goggles, a bag of golf clubs, a sweater, six tennis balls, a bathroom, with needle shower (exclusive), a bathrobe, a pair of slippers, a pair of tennis shoes, a bathing suit, a box of cigarettes (fifty in a box), a set of diabolo sticks, a riding and driving horse, a fur overcoat, an umbrella, a bottle of eau de cologne, and a box of postage stamps.

GUESTS are always invited from Friday night to Monday morning. It is wiser for the hostess to mention the Monday trains, or one of the guests may decide to stop longer. This is seldom a wise plan. Hostesses should clear the house of all guests before the three-day limit. Remember the Spanish proverb, "El huesped y el pece à tres dias hiede," which, being translated, means, "Any guest, like any fish, is bound to be objectionable on the third day."

IN certain country houses the architect has neglected to supply bathrooms for each of the guests. In some extreme cases as many as three bachelors are expected to share one bath. This is bad.

The best way to maneuver under such circumstances is to send your servant early to the bathroom and let him lock himself in. This will foil the invaders. When he hears your special knock on the door, he can open to you, and you can then bathe, take a nap in the bath, shave, smoke a cigarette, and read the papers in quiet.

AT a house party every lady of prominence is sure to bring at least one Pomeranian dog. Many think it wiser to bring a black and a brown, so that, no matter what gown they may wear, one of the darlings is sure not to clash with it. These pets are, of course, extremely expensive. A smart week-end on the Hudson will usually average about six thousand dollars' worth of Poms.

※

IN nearly all guest rooms the hostess is sure to provide white enamel writing desks, chiffoniers, and tables. By leaving lighted cigarettes on such articles of furniture you are almost certain to secure a very curious and amusing stain, or burn. Sometimes, if your visit is long enough, you can etch, in this way, a complete pattern around a fair-sized table. The Greek fret and egg-and-dart designs are neat and extremely popular.

※

THE passage through a country house of the framed photograph of a friend is often an instructive spectacle to witness. Such a trophy usually begins its career in the drawing-room. It is then moved to the library, and subsequently to the smoking room. After that it begins a heavenly flight into one of the guest rooms, from which place it ascends on its last earthly pilgrimage to the attic.

THE English have rather a clever way of "chucking" a week-end engagement in the country. They merely telegraph as follows:

"Impossible to come to-day: lie follows by mail."

AN unprotected lady should be careful not to employ convivial or tippling butlers. We are acquainted with a widow who was recently petrified with horror when her drunken butler entered her sleeping apartment in the dead of the night and proceeded to lay the table for six—upon her bed.

MANNERS *for the* METROPOLIS

SUNDAY morning in the country is usually rainy. This is invariably the fault of the hostess. When you descend in the morning, look at her reproachfully; mention the rain; remark on the fact that it has *always* rained when you have visited her before; sink hopelessly on a sofa, and sigh.

HOSTESSES very often have a distressing way of asking you how you slept. Under such circumstances it is permissible to speak the truth and to mention, quite frankly, the mosquitoes and the topographical whimsicalities of your bed.

IN a country house, if you find, on going up to your room to dress for dinner, that no studs have been put into your evening shirt, complain at once to the stud groom.

BEWARE of inviting fashionable bachelors for the week-end unless you maintain an adequate *ménage*. The recent and distressing case of a lady (with but one spare room and a very small establishment) may serve as a terrible example.

Her visitor arrived rather late on a rainy night. His belongings looked like those of a traveling theatrical company, and included one forty horse power Mercedes car, a Swiss valet, a violin case, one trunk, two hat boxes, five pounds of bonbons, a fur overcoat, a photographic camera, a bag of golf clubs, a talking machine, two boxes of health cocoa, an Austrian chauffeur, an oxygen jar, two polo ponies, an air cushion, a wire-haired fox terrier, and a box of one hundred clay pigeons.

CONVERSATION

THE conversation at a club should be simple and conventional. It is vulgar to go into long or prolix discussions. Only a few remarks are *comme il faut*, such as "Hello!" "Deuced cold!" "Have a drink?" "Who has a cigar?" "How about one rubber?"

Perhaps the safest and most refined remark for constant use is: "Waiter, take the orders." Even this may be dispensed with—if you make certain to ring the bell.

※

IT is not modish to speak kindly to the servants either in your own or in other people's houses. In addressing them, simply say:

"A napkin," "The cigars," "Where the devil are my boots?" Remember that they "get even" in the servants' hall.

IT is customary, in alluding to ladies in the ultra-fashionable set (provided they are not present) to speak of them by their pet names: "Birdie," "Baby," "Tessie," "Posy"; but, when face to face with these ladies, the utmost formality had best be observed.

IN criticising a play or a novel be careful to avoid long and discriminating criticisms. You should either "knock" or "boost." Try to remember that there are only two kinds of plays or novels—they are either "bully" or "rotten."

IF a few people in the smart set are entertaining a stranger at lunch, it is *de rigueur* for them to converse with each other entirely in whispers and always on subjects with which he is absolutely unfamiliar.

IN discussing literature at a lunch or dinner, try to remember that there are but a very few fashionable authors. They are as follows: Mrs. Wharton, Colonel Mann, Mrs. Glyn, Robert Hichens, F. Peter Dunne, John Fox, Jr., and Billy Baxter.

AT a dinner a gentleman sitting beside a débutante should congratulate her upon her début, and, in a few well-chosen words, should discuss the usual débutante topics—

i. e., platonic love, banting, Ethel Barrymore, French dressmakers, John Drew, the relative merits of Harvard and Yale, love at first sight, the football match and the matter of her great personal beauty and charm.

Try always to remember that the chief and most interesting topics of conversation are herself and yourself. *Serious* topics are very properly deemed out of place in society.

AFTER dinner, over the cigars, it is bad form for men to discuss any subjects but stocks and motor cars.

WHENEVER, at a dinner, an anecdote is narrated in French, it is always a wise precaution to laugh heartily.

WOMEN should not complain of their husbands in public. All married women have a great deal to contend with. Everybody knows that married men make very poor husbands.

AT a dinner the safest conversational opening is as follows: " Is that your bread, or mine ? "

WHEN, at a dinner, you don't know the lady next to you, show her your dinner card and say:

" I'm that; what are you ? "

CHIVALRY demands that a lady's name should never be mentioned in a gentleman's club. Occasionally, however, this hard-and-fast rule may be slightly infracted, and her intimate affairs discreetly talked over—provided that the group of gentlemen be a small one and absolute privacy assured.

N. B.—A " small group " is any group of less than twelve.

DINNERS

DINNERS

A DINNER is a miscellaneous collection of appropriately dressed men and women, who are not in the least hungry and who are invited by the host and hostess to repay certain social obligations for value received or expected. The attitude of the guests at such a repast is very often one of regret and revolt, because of the haunting memory of an invitation, much more enticing in its prospects, but, alas, more recently received.

✻

ON arriving at a dinner a servant should hand each male guest an envelope containing a card. This card will bear the name of the lady whom he is to take in to dinner. This part of the ceremony is usually accompanied by groans and maledictions as the gentlemen tremblingly open their envelopes.

Some hostesses allow their guests to file in to dinner in ignorance of their partners. They thus learn their fate at the dinner table, which postpones the terrible shock for as long a period as possible.

NOTHING adds so much to an appearance of *savoir faire* as the art of gracefully removing from a dinner or evening party a gentleman who has imbibed, not wisely but too well. The correct method is to ask the butler to inform him that a lady wishes to speak to him on the telephone. When he has left the room, spring upon him in the hall and chivy him into a cab.

Rouge sticks and powder puffs may be used by ladies at luncheons, but *never* at dinners.

If a bachelor receives a dinner invitation from people who are not really "in the swim" (people, let us say, like old friends, classmates, and business associates, who are, so to speak, "on the green, but not dead to the hole"), he should simply toss it into the fire. This plan will prevent any more invitations from so undesirable a quarter. Were he to answer these people politely, they would certainly annoy him again at a later date. Remember that "the coward does it with a kiss, the brave man with a sword."

Do not address your best thoughts to the ladies until they have had an opportunity to brush the glove powder from their arms and to look carefully at the dresses and ornaments of the other ladies at the dinner.

※

AT a very large dinner, the lady beside you is almost certain to be one who entertains generously and, as such, should be treated with a certain degree of politeness. Try to suppress, however, all sentiments purely human in their nature, such as pity, kindness of heart, sympathy, enthusiasm, love of books, music, and art.

These ridiculous sentiments are in exceedingly bad taste and should be used but sparingly, if at all.

※

LADIES do not call upon a bachelor, in his rooms, after attending a dinner given by him—except in Mrs. Wharton's novels.

ON leaving a dinner you should always manage to come down the steps with a group of the super-rich—they may give you a lift home.

※

ON driving home with friends from a dinner, it is the generally accepted practice to abuse the host and draw particular attention to his ghastly collection of family portraits, his wretched plate, and execrable food. Do not fail also to draw a moving picture of the stupidity and hideousness of the lady next to you at dinner—unless she should be in the carriage with you at the time.

※

WHEN you are over half an hour late at a dinner it is well to have an excuse. There are, just now, only two modish excuses:

First, you were arrested for speeding your motor; second, you were playing bridge, and every hand seemed to be a spade or a club.

WHEN a gentleman at a dinner upsets a plate of terrapin, a ruddy duck, or a bowl of vegetable salad upon the dress of the lady beside him, she should laugh merrily and should always be provided with some apt jest with which to carry off the little *contretemps*.

FLETCHERITES have lately added a new horror to dining out. These strange creatures seldom repay attention. The best that can be expected from them is the tense and awful silence which always accompanies their excruciating tortures of mastication.

MANNERS *for the* METROPOLIS

THERE are two *recherché* methods for a bachelor to refuse a verbal dinner invitation. The first is to say that you are dining with a business associate. The second is to say that your engagement book is at home and that you will consult it immediately upon reaching there and will telephone. This gives you the desired opportunity of saying " No." It is always easier over the wire than face to face.

IN wriggling out of a dinner at the last moment in New York, it is *chic* to invent some mythical female relative in Philadelphia who has developed a sudden and alarming illness and has hastily summoned you to her bedside.

IF, at a dinner, food is passed to you which you do not care to eat, it is good form to

✽

AFTER dinner, if a lady has been asked to sing and refused, do not urge her further. It is the height of bad manners, and there is just the off chance that she may yield.

✽

IN England the matter of precedence at dinners is simplicity itself. The Sovereign precedes an ambassador, who precedes the Archbishop of Canterbury, who precedes the Earl Marshal, who precedes a duke, who precedes an earl, a marquis, a viscount, a bishop, a baron, etc.; but in America the matter is a much more perplexing one.

The author of this *brochure* respectfully suggests the following scheme of American dinner precedence: Let an opera box count 6 points; steam yacht, 5; town house, 5; country house, 4; motors, 3 each; every million dollars, 2; tiara, 1; good wine cellar, 1; ballroom in town house, 1; a known grandparent of either sex, $\frac{1}{2}$; culture, $\frac{1}{8}$. By this system, a woman of culture with four known grandparents and a million dollars will have a total of $4\frac{1}{8}$. She will, of course, be forced to follow in the wake of a lady with a town house and a tiara (6); who, in turn, will trail after a woman with a steam yacht and two motors (11). The highest known total is about 100; the lowest, about $\frac{1}{8}$. The housekeeper may arrange the totals, and the hostess can then send the guests in according to their listed quotations.

PEOPLE who arrive late at a large dinner sometimes have very quaint and amusing excuses. A hostess at a recent eight-o'clock banquet collected the following gems:

I overslept in my bath.

A cinder lodged in my eye and I have just come from the chemist's.

My maid is ill and I was forced to hook myself.

The twins put crumbs in my stockings.

I read your invitation upside down and, naturally, mistook the hour of dinner.

I never eat soup, and thought, of course, you wouldn't wait.

I knew Mrs. V——t would be *much* later than I—so I took a chance.

I was taking my memory lesson, and it was all so absorbing that I completely forgot the dinner.

I lost your note, and, as *everybody* dines at 8.30, I thought, of course, that *you* would.

My chauffeur was so drunk that he took me next door by mistake, and delayed me fearfully.

EVERY year it is becoming more and more difficult for hostesses to secure a sufficient number of blades for their dinners and evening routs. "Odd men" are always in tremendous demand.

The custom of shouting names, which is imperfectly followed at the hotels, should be perfected in our clubs, and we hope soon to see the club waiters wandering about the halls and lounging rooms shouting out, as they go: "Mrs. Vanderlip, four odd men for dinner." "Mrs. Miles, two bachelors for the opera." "Mrs. Nestor, one married couple for bridge," etc.

WHEN a lady beside you is so generously avoirdupoised or embonpointed that it is a physical impossibility for her to see the food upon her plate, it is sometimes an act of kindness to inform her as to the nature of the bird or beast so hopelessly removed from her vision. This saves her the trouble of lifting it above the horizon in order to discover its exact species.

A CLEVER hostess in New York has recently trained a highly intelligent dachshund to fly about after dinner, under the banquet table, and fetch out the long white gloves, make-up boxes, scarves, and lace handkerchiefs. Most hostesses, however, prefer to put their guests on the scent and let them retrieve the hidden treasures.

A FRANTIC hostess recently telephoned us for advice on a nice point of social etiquette. She had arranged a dinner of twelve, and was confronted and confounded, at the last moment, by an "odd" bachelor whom she had originally invited and subsequently forgotten. She could not sit down thirteen at the table.

"What shall I do?" she asked.

We were glad to be able to come to the distressed lady's assistance and telephoned her as follows:

"You should hand him a neatly folded dollar bill and ask him to slip out quietly and buy himself a good dinner at a corner restaurant. Your butler may also give him a cigar as he passes into the night."

IF you are giving a supper after the play, it is *de rigueur* to order grape fruit, hot bouillon, champagne, birds, a salad, and a sweet. The sated guests will not touch any of the food, but it is *comme il faut* to put it all before them.

B‍ANTING has almost done away with the ancient custom of eating, but thyroid tablets and lemon juice are, of course, permitted. At a ladies' lunch the guests (whether ladies, millionairesses, or workingwomen) should be careful disdainfully to dismiss the dainty dishes until the repast is over, when they should look benignly at the hostess and murmur:

"Dear Mrs. Brown—*might* I have a cup of very hot water?"

W‍HEN a lady must pay back forty dinner obligations and her dining room will seat only twenty, it is obvious that she must have two dinners of twenty each. She should give the feasts on successive evenings, as the left-over flowers, bonbons, fruits, and *pâtés* will always do service at the second repast.

MANNERS *for the* METROPOLIS

A LADY should be careful not to turn to the gentleman beside her and complain of the " fizz." There is always a good chance that he is the wine agent.

※

WHEN, in New York, a married couple do not pull along together, and have definitely decided to divorce or separate, it is customary for them once or twice to dine, *tête-à-tête*, at Sherry's: to flirt, laugh, and make merry with each other—in order to put the eager hounds off the scent.

※

AT dinners in the *beau monde* the footmen will invariably pounce upon your plate and run off with it before you have half finished the course. Be careful not to hold on to it like a despairing mother whose child is being torn from her arms, as such scenes at table are always deplorable and harassing.

IN purchasing almond bonbons for the dinner table the hostess should make sure to select the mauve species. No one ever eats them. A dishful of the white variety will sometimes vanish in a night, but the mauve go on forever.

DANCES

IN New York the word "ball" is intended to signify a hundred or so people who do not care particularly for dancing, who are prostrated by the prospect of arising early on the following morning, and who leave their cotillion favors untouched and disregarded upon the gilt chairs in the ballroom.

The chief characteristics of a ball may be summed up, briefly, as follows: Mothers, or "benchwomen," wildly eying their offspring; the "leader," battered and bruised like a half-back in a football game; the hostess, with her tiara aslant on her new false curls; fifty wilted linen collars; fifty ditto shirts; four red-faced gentlemen asleep in the smoking room; the host leaping from train to train with the agility of a brakeman; two hundred yards of chiffon ruffles and one pound of assorted hairpins decorating the floor of the ballroom; a deep crowd of so-called dancing men who effectually block the entrance door and stand in a dazed and awkward group, spellbound by the horrors of the scene.

THE valuable checks for cotillion seats are usually cornered by the cotillion leader and dealt out to the most prominent tiaras. The unhappy ladies who fail to receive one of these priceless tokens usually pass the remainder of the evening in the ultimate row of chairs wearing a granite smile and a paper cotillion favor.

A WALL flower is a young lady at a dance who has not been cursed with the fatal gift.

MANNERS *for the* METROPOLIS

She may usually be distinguished by her wild and beseeching glances. Chloroform is the only possible way of securing a partner for her.

⁂

BEFORE putting your arm around a lady's waist, you should explain to her that it is your intention to dance. As the music starts, look at her longingly and murmur one of the following remarks: " Do you Boston? " " Rotten floor " (or) " Bully floor." " Bully favors " (or) " Rotten favors."

⁂

EVERY now and then a "stand-up" supper is served at a dance. This is the abomination of desolation spoken of by the prophet Daniel. Should a lady ask you at such an entertainment to get her some supper, push your

MANNERS *for the* METROPOLIS

way through the mob of angry bachelors to the trough where the comestibles are displayed. Once arrived on the scene of carnage, you can consume a cup of bouillon, a few oysters, some sandwiches, a little chicken, some dry champagne, a plate of salad, an ice, and a cup of coffee. After this, if your hunger has been satisfied, take a morsel of *galantine*, a doily, and a lady-finger, place them on a plate and force yourself through the compact lines of angry, feeding, perspiring " dancing men," until you appear before your fair partner, declaring that you did your best, and that the rest of the provisions had disappeared. While she is thanking you, slip away to the smoking room and send the man in attendance there for a bottle of some very, very old champagne. While he is gone you may busy yourself by selecting a few of the best cigars, so as to be sure to have something to smoke on the way home—in somebody's cab.

IN giving a dance, avoid, *if possible*, sending invitations to bores—they come without them.

AT a dance, when a lady is talking to a millionaire recently arrived from the West, he may offer to introduce his wife. (This is part of what, in sporting circles, is known as the "push stroke.") In such a fix it is permissible for her to burst into a loud fit of coughing, mention her weak heart, and ask a footman to call her carriage.

WHEN a bachelor arrives at a dance, he should at once repair to the smoking room and remain there most of the evening—calling loudly for all those wines which his host has neglected to provide.

A NEW and unspeakable horror has lately been introduced into fashionable dances in New York—namely, the "third supper." The writer is glad to say that the inventor of this atrocity died very slowly and in great pain about a year ago. It is a comfort to know that his last resting place is unadorned by any monument, and that no flowers or shrubs have ever bloomed upon his grave.

※

A POPULAR form of entertainment for grown-up persons in New York is a "baby party." Here the guests are dressed like babies: they dance and have supper, and are permitted to behave like little children. These revels do not differ from other forms of social festivities in the metropolis—except as regards the costumes.

DANCING men should have a care, at a ball, never to be "stuck." This catastrophe is usually brought about by listening to the wiles of a man who begins with some such remark as "Do you know Miss A——? She is crazy to meet you!" or "For Heaven's sake, dear boy, *do* go and talk to that unfortunate girl in yellow."

Many an agonized hour may be avoided by turning a deaf ear to all such entreaties. If you don't, the horror of your ultimate predicament can hardly be exaggerated. You will sit with her for hours in isolated agony. Slowly your hair will turn as white as the driven snow. Interminable cycles of time will tick themselves away, while you sit there slyly beckoning to other gentlemen who are certain to pay no heed to your signals.

A case is on record, in England, where a gentleman, in such a position, addressed no remark to his partner for upward of three hours. At this point she became aweary, turned, and found that he was—dead!

※

A VERY neat trick can sometimes be worked at a dance. You have steadily avoided a particularly dreadful damsel throughout the entire evening. When she has put on her cloak and fur overshoes, and you see her hurrying through the hall with her maid, on her way to her carriage, jump out of the smoking room and say:

"What? Home so early! Can't you stay and have *just* one with me?"

Be careful, of course, not to be too urgent, else she may stay, thus hoisting you on your own petard.

※

IN dancing, unless you are an accomplished waltzer, the safest advice to follow is: "Avoid the corners and keep kicking."

Hostess

AT a large ball, the hostess, when tired, may, with perfect safety, go to her sleeping apartment and retire for an hour or two. No one will ever miss her. When rested she can reappear in the ballroom and, with her second wind, as it were, enjoy the third supper, or the first breakfast.

IN saying good night to the hostess, have a care to bestow your avowals of obligation in nearly the same degree of warmth or formality that her bearing invites. If, for instance, she be asleep in the conservatory, all among the begonias, it is not necessary to shake her or rouse her by shouting: "Hi! Wake up, I want to go home," etc. Simply pass out noiselessly and remind her butler to call her in time for breakfast. (See the illustration, "Hostess.")

BRIDGE

BRIDGE

This is a popular pastime, and much of the attention of our best minds in high society is concentrated upon guessing whether a given card is in the hand of the person on the right or on the left.

As there is a great curiosity among all classes of readers concerning bridge, the benevolent author has gone into the etiquette of the game with a good deal of thoroughness.

In order to be an accomplished bridge player one must possess the following attributes:

A dress suit. (This does not apply to ladies.)

A large roll of clean bills with a rubber band encircling them.

A cigarette and ash tray.

A stoical, blond and unimpassioned nature.

A partner—usually of the opposite sex.

You may, with safety, criticise nearly every play your fair partner makes. She doubtless deserves it, but, as a rule, this criticism should not extend beyond her faults *as a player*. Try to remember that a [gentleman is one who never unintentionally insults anybody.]

Bridge should never be played seriously. One should carry on an animated conversation during the course of play. It is customary, too, to hold the cards in one hand and a hot buttered muffin in the other. Get up from the table rather frequently and telephone, receive visitors, give orders to the servants, and pour tea. The questions, "Who led?" "What are trumps?" "Is that our trick?" etc., are always permissible, and lend some spirit to what might otherwise prove a dull and taxing game.

IN playing bridge with two ladies, a man should be careful to play "highest man and highest woman." In this way he will be playing against a man, and his chances of a "settlement" will be a little less remote. Never play with three ladies.

WHEN you are dummy and your partner has finished playing the hand, you should invariably glare at her (or him) and make one of the following remarks:

You played it the only way to lose the odd!

Why, in Heaven's name, didn't you get out the trumps?

You must lose a pot of money at this game, don't you?

It's lucky I'm not playing ten-cent points.

Why not take your finesse the other way?

The eight of clubs was good, you know!

Yes, if you had played your ace of diamonds we would have saved it.

It's a pity you didn't open the hearts.

※

As the leaders of the Smart Set have ceased occupying their brains with literature, music, politics, and art—subjects which were, a long time ago, discussed in our best society—and as their entire mental activities are now focused upon the game of bridge, the author has added for the further benefit of his readers a series of anecdotes, maxims, and experiences which he has gathered during his fruitless attempts to master this fashionable pastime.

※

THERE was a lady in the *beau monde* of New York who was not only a charming woman but an accomplished whist player. Unfortunately, however, she simply *could* not play fair. Among other idiosyncrasies she had a distressing habit of slipping a high card on the bottom of the pack, after the cut—this was in the days when she played old-fashioned whist. In this way she was always certain of the ace, king, or queen of trumps when it was her turn to deal. She was detected in this graceful little artifice on one or two occasions, with the result that her reputation suffered a slight dimming in its glory.

A few months ago the poor lady died and

"Here lies Lily Maltravers,
In confident expectation of
The last trump."

※

A DELIGHTFUL bridge player is Mrs. R. U. Rich, who, though stone deaf, still manages to understand the declarations, or makes, by an elaborate series of manual signs. In playing with her, if the make is a heart, you must point to your heart; diamonds, to your ring; spades, you must make a shovel of your hand, and, when clubs have been declared, you must shake your fist at her. The other evening at a fashionable house in New York she was playing a rubber in which her husband was her partner. It was after a large dinner and, Mrs. Rich, having mistaken her husband's signal, excitedly asked him what trump had been declared. At this, her better half shook his fist at her two or three times in a very convincing way. An elderly lady, on the other side of the room, unaware of Mrs. Rich's infirmity, gathered her dress about her and, with great dignity, begged the host to send for her carriage.

"Why, Mrs. ——," he said, "are you leaving us so early?"

"Well," said the lady of the old school, "I think that when a husband and wife come to blows over the bridge table it is time to call the carriages."

※

A REDUCED gentlewoman, living in a small way in the suburbs, was at an employment agency trying to secure a cook. As the lady and her husband lived some distance from any neighbor, and as the wages she could afford to pay were meager, the cooks displayed a decided unwillingness to assume the cares of office.

Finally, to the great elation of the lady, a very respectable and well-mannered English girl seemed disposed to risk the rigors of suburban life. The searching questions which the girl had put to the lady had been satisfactorily answered, when, at the very last, she asked the number in the family, to which the lady replied that there were only two—herself and her husband.

"Oh!" said the girl, "I could not *think* of going into service with only three in the house. I would not work *anywhere* unless we could make up a four at bridge."

HUSBANDS and wives should never play partners at bridge. They are almost certain to quarrel, which is unseemly—and if they *don't* quarrel, their friends are sure to suspect them of collusion and cheating.

⁂

IT is a mistake for parents to play bridge on Sunday. The morals of children should ever be sacred in a parent's eye. Never, therefore, allow a card to be touched on the Sabbath—until the children have gone to bed.

⁂

AN inveterate bridge fiend recently proposed to a lady of some means. She, doubting his entire sincerity, mentioned his too great devotion to bridge. With a fine show of enthusiasm and erudition he burst out with:

> "I could not love thee, dear, so much,
> Loved I not honors more."

THERE is always a great deal of discussion among good bridge players as to the propriety of an original club make—with no score. As a matter of fact, a big club hand is usually disastrous whether you make it or pass it. You either leave it and get spades, or else you *don't* leave it and get the devil.

※

THERE is a lady in New York society who is as devoted to bridge as one could well be. She makes everything, except her two children, subservient to the game. She attends bridge classes, bridge teas, and bridge tournaments without end. She is, unfortunately, married to a wealthy but worthless and rascally young clubman who treats her usually with indifference, but sometimes with cruelty.

Her friends all advised her to sue for a divorce.

The poor woman was in some doubt as to what course to pursue. Finally, a brilliant idea occurred to her. She would consult her bridge teacher! He was the one man in all the world whose judgment seemed to her infallible. She trusted him more than she did her lawyer or her minister. He had solved so many difficult problems for her that he might solve this.

Mr. Elstreet was accordingly written to by the unhappy lady. His answer ran as follows:

> My dear Mrs.———:
>
> I have very carefully thought over the little problem which you were good enough to submit to me for solution. It seems to me that when you have a knave alone, it is often a wise plan to discard him, but holding, as you do, a knave and two little ones, it would seem the better part of discretion not to discard him.
>
> I am, my dear Mrs. ———, yours, etc.

A WELL-KNOWN widow in London was a guest at a large house-party. She was an enthusiastic bridger. She took the game very seriously—so seriously that she frequently dreamed about it, and even, her maid declared, talked about it in her sleep.

Everybody had been playing fairly late and the ladies had gone to their rooms and "turned in" at about twelve o'clock. The men had played until about two. Shortly after this, the housekeeper, in making her final round of the house, was startled to hear the widow's voice addressing somebody in an agonized and supplicating way.

As the door of the widow's room was ajar, the housekeeper paused in some alarm, only to hear her call out: "My diamonds, my diamonds, why didn't I protect them? I am lost, absolutely lost!"

The housekeeper, not knowing the intricacies of bridge and thoroughly alarmed by the idea of a burglar in the widow's room, rushed to the host's door and hastily summoned him to the rescue. After a somewhat noisy consultation between them, as a result of which some of the disrobing bachelors were attracted to the scene of conflict, a united descent was made upon the unfortunate widow's stronghold. The net result of the *sortie* was that the widow was greatly annoyed, the host was unmercifully chaffed, and the housekeeper received her first lesson in bridge.

"IT was," said the Knickerbocker bridge fiend, "at the Hotel Splendide-Royale in Aix-les-Bains. I was playing twenty-cent points, which is just double my usual limit. I had lost six consecutive rubbers. I had cut, each rubber, against a peculiarly malevolent-looking Spaniard, who had a reputation at cards which was none too savory. There had been trouble about him only the day before at the Casino des Fleurs, where he had been mixed up in a somewhat unpleasant baccarat scandal. He was a crafty and sullen bridge player and I had conceived a most cordial dislike to him.

"Finally—it was hideously late and the card-room waiter was snoring in the service closet—my time for revenge arrived. It was my deal, and I saw at a glance that I had dealt myself an enormous hand. I could hardly believe my eyes. I held nine spades with the four top honors, the bare ace of clubs, the bare ace of hearts, and the king and queen of diamonds. Here was a certainty of eleven tricks at no trumps and very possibly twelve or thirteen. I looked at the Spaniard, whose turn it was to lead, and I smiled exultantly.

"'No trumps,' I said, the note of triumph quite perceptible in my voice. Quick as a

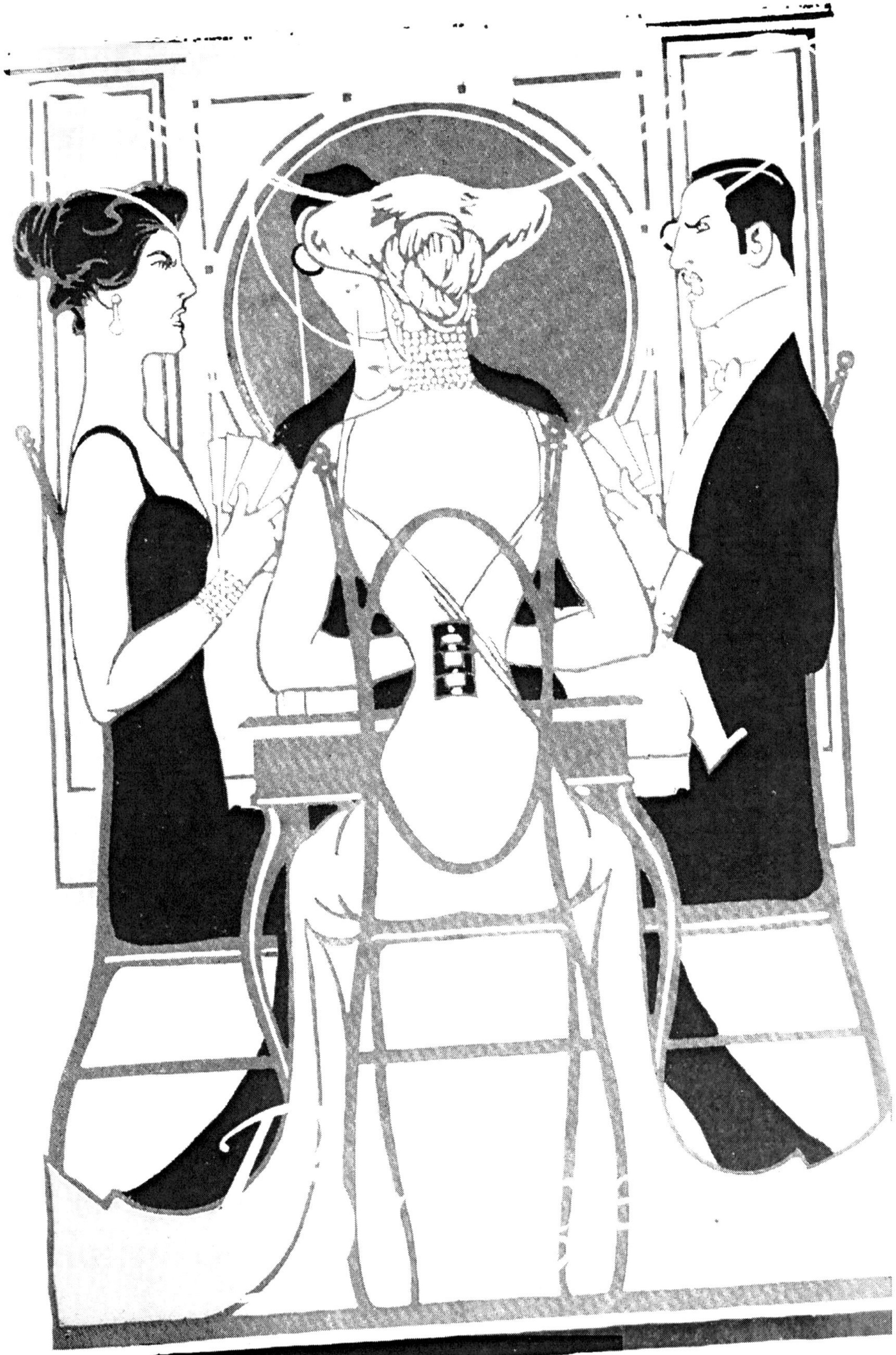

flash the Spaniard had doubled—and quick as another I had redoubled.

"When, however, he had jacked it up to 96 a trick, I hesitated, but of course went at him again with 192. 'Ah, ha!' I said to myself, 'Mr. bird of ill omen, you are my prey, my chosen victim for the sacrifice.'

"The price per trick had soon sailed up to 1,536, and I ventured to look at my partner. He was chalky white about the gills and his eyes seemed to stare idiotically into space. His expression prompted me to take pity on him and say 'enough.'

"Suddenly I had a terrible feeling of alarm. Had I mistaken the queen of diamonds for the queen of hearts? If so, my king of diamonds was bare and the mysterious Spaniard might run off twelve diamond tricks before I could say 'Jack Robinson.' With a sinking heart I looked at my hand again—all was well! The queen was surely a diamond. I glanced at the olive-skinned gentleman and begged him to lead a card. I felt a great joy welling up within me.

"At this moment the Spaniard led a card and I looked at it nervously. As soon as my eyes beheld it my heart seemed to stop beating. He had opened the ace of a strange green suit, a suit which I had never seen before, a suit all covered with mysterious figures and symbols. I felt strangely giddy but discarded a low spade. I looked at my partner, who was the picture of despair. He said, mechanically and as though life had lost all beauty for him, 'Having no hyppogryphs?' to which icy inquiry I answered in a strange whisper, 'No gryppolyphs.'

"The leader followed with another green card, a king this time, and again I sacrificed another beautiful spade. The Spaniard smiled a mahogany smile and proceeded to run off his entire suit of thirteen green cards. He then nonchalantly scored up a grand slam, the game, and a rubber of 10,450 points or

$2,090. I felt my brain reeling and fainted away with my head on the card table. Very soon, however, I thought I felt the Spaniard tugging at my coat sleeve. My anger at this was beyond all bounds. I opened my eyes, prepared to strike the crafty foreigner in his wicked face, and saw—my servant standing by my bed with my breakfast tray in his hands and my bathrobe on his arm."

THE THEATER

At the theater it is smart to "roast the show." Do not be afraid of wounding the feelings of your host and hostess. It is an even chance that they are more bored than you. If the actors seem to object to your conversation or show annoyance or impatience, try to remember that they are not, as a rule, well bred, and are ignorant of all the graceful little social conventions.

On leaving the opera with ladies, do not go into the draughty side corridors with them, or you will surely be forced to look out for their carriage, a tedious and bothersome occupation. The wisest thing to do is to say that you have an appointment, and merge yourself with the rabble who are leaving by the front door, allowing the ladies to remain in the side corridors, where their footmen will sooner or later discover them.

NEVER give a theater party in stalls. Boxes are obligatory. In seats, the men cannot go out for refreshment, and the ladies are forced to remove their hats, a tragedy usually accompanied by the most distressing and ignominious disclosures.

LADIES who have opera boxes given them at the last moment should "get on the job" at once and offer it to such of their friends as they know to be either out of town or engaged for that evening. A box has been known, under such circumstances, to pay off a dozen obligations in a single day.

※

IN New York a theater party is often a very boring and tedious form of revelry. It is always wise to send a "feeler" before accepting a lady's invitation to dine and go to the play. The following is a safe model for such a missive:

> MY DEAR MRS. VANDERGRAFT:
> How awfully good of you to ask me for Friday. I presume we are dining at your house and not at a stuffy restaurant. May I be very frank and ask you what play you are planning to see? Might I also inquire if you are going in boxes or seats, and if you expect me for supper afterwards?
> On hearing from you, I hope to be

able to arrange the matter to your entire satisfaction.

My servant will wait for your reply.
Sincerely yours,
REGINALD GOOLD.

P. S.—How many are coming, and who are they? Are they the noisy sort?

P. S. No. 2.—What ladies are to sit beside me at dinner?

CALLING

CALLING

BACHELORS no longer leave or " push " cards. It is considered provincial. After dining at a house, a man may think it policy to give the butler two dollars and his card. In return the butler will, during the next afternoon, discreetly slip the card upon the tray in the hall while the lady of the house is driving in the park.

IF you are literally forced to pay a call, merely ask the butler if the ladies are at home. Should he say " No," hand him your cards, and your work is over. Should he say " Yes," pretend to him that you have mistaken the house, and that you were looking for the residence of another lady. Slip him a dollar and retire noiselessly down the steps.

*

It is often well, before starting out on a calling expedition, to have one's servant telephone to a dozen or so mansions to discover which of the ladies are out. You can then leave cards in these particular houses with comparative safety.

OUR COUNTRY COUSINS

OUR COUNTRY COUSINS

GREEN peas are eaten with the aid of a fork. The hair-raising spectacle of a gentleman flicking peas into his mouth with a steel knife is no longer fashionable, however dexterously the feat may be performed.

PLUMS should be eaten one by one and the pits allowed to fall noiselessly into the half-closed hand.

AT dinners, wisdom dictates that it is wiser to leave the terrapin, hard crabs, asparagus, and oranges untasted (unless accustomed to them from birth). Be content to poke and pat these dishes with a fork, but make no effort to consume them.

⁂

THE following expressions are no longer in vogue in society: "Pardon my glove," "Pray be seated," "Pleased to meet you," "Remember me to the folks," "Pray rest your cane," "Make yourself at home," "What name, please?" "Are you the party?" "Say, listen," "My gentleman friend," "Usen't you?" etc.

⁂

DO not address your wife as "mother."

⁂

OLIVES are eaten with the thumb and forefinger of the right hand. It is not necessary to peel them, and the pits should usually be rejected.

Do not, when your mouth is filled with sweet potatoes, red bananas, pressed saddle of lamb, or other solid provisions, attempt to discuss the topics of the day with the ladies at the feast.

In using a finger bowl, simply dip the index finger into the fluid and pass it lightly over the lips.

Make no effort to consume the floating lemon, and try to restrain yourself from splashing about in the bath, like a playful walrus or a performing seal.

When a rich Westerner arrives in New York and begins breaking into society, it should be a pleasure for everybody to show him little courtesies and attentions. New York gentlemen usually do this by borrowing money from him, marrying his daughters, riding his polo ponies (or selling him theirs), drinking his wine, cruising about on his yacht, smoking his cigars, and selling him blocks of their worthless stocks.

※

THE last morsel of green turtle in a soup plate is always a heart-breaking thing at best. Remember that, though enticing, it is elusive. Do not chivy it about in frantic circles or pursue it untiringly around your plate until you have captured and subdued it. Turtle soup and Indian pig-sticking are not governed by the same rules.

※

WHEN you sit down at table, it is not necessary to whisk the napkin gayly about before unfolding it. The concealed roll is certain to fly a considerable distance before alighting, and may even crack the enameling on one of the great ladies at the banquet.

MILLIONAIRES of the Chester A. Arthur or Rutherford B. Hayes vintage should pass rapidly through their ancient mansions and demolish the following objects of art and *vertu*:

The twin conch shells, for fireside use; the embroidered wall mottoes; imitation wax flowers—under glass; ebony and gold whatnots; velvet antimacassars; all crayon portraits—whether pendant or on gold easels; party-colored crazy quilts; all magenta picture sashes; plush photograph albums; red worm lamp-mats; turkish cozy corners, with hanging red lamps, imitation spears, and rusty armor; black hair sofas; hanging tennis racquets ornamented with red bows; folding beds; cuckoo clocks and paper weights containing miniature paper snowstorms.

After destroying these knickknacks, they should pass out on the steps and adjacent lawn spaces and demolish the iron dogs, copper fauns, and the bed of snowdrops spelling out the mansion's fantastic name—"Slopeoak," "Munnysunk," "Sewerside," or any name in which the following popular "B" forms are included: Brae, Blythe, By-the, Buena, Bel, Bonnie, Beau, Bourne.

NEWPORT

The correct treatment of a foreigner in Newport is to gush over him, praise him to your friends, and invite him to your entertainments. This course may be pursued for one week. After that, treat him with great reserve and coolness for the same period of time. At the beginning of the third week you should abuse him roundly, and take pains to recite the hidden and secret passages of his past. Advice for the fourth week is unnecessary: they never last more than three.

※

Sea bathing at Newport is often injurious to the health, as in the case of those ladies

MANNERS *for the* METROPOLIS

whose figures are a trifle too meagre—or too ample. To such sirens the doctor is sure to forbid it. Where, however, the outlines are visually "grateful and comforting," the exercise is certain to prove beneficial and bracing. In all Newport there are about a dozen ladies whose physicians have no such prejudices against open air, salt water bathing.

※

DAKOTA divorces are still a good deal frowned upon in the *beau monde*. Try to remember that only Rhode Island divorces are *comme il faut*. (The Newport variety is far smarter than the Providence or Bristol brand.) Dakota divorces are a trifle cheaper and more expeditious, but it should be borne in mind that the climate of Sioux Falls is very variable and that the hotels and theaters are, to say the least, indifferent.

MANNERS *for the* METROPOLIS

MILLIONAIRES from the West whose wives are bent upon breaking into society at any cost, should not try Newport until the simpler safes have been cracked. Newport is the water jump of the social steeplechase, and should not be taken until the easier gates have been successfully negotiated. The safest graded order of jumps is as follows:

1. PALM BEACH. Not exclusive, but merry, sumptuous, and expensive. Chance to meet many smart men in the gambling rooms.
2. HOT SPRINGS, VA. Depressing, but many "classy" invalids.
3. NARRAGANSETT PIER. Geographically speaking, this is nearly Newport,

but the social tone, though "nobby," can hardly be called A1.

4. THE BERKSHIRES. Dull and dowdy, but full of genteel old families in reduced circumstances who are willing to unbend—if properly propitiated.

5. TUXEDO. Excellent opportunities here, particularly in the Tuxedo jiggers and at the club on rainy days, when a fourth is needed at bridge.

6. LONG ISLAND. This is the Tattenham Corner of

the social Derby —(many bad falls here—due to riding too hard) —the last great turn before the finish. (Try Hempstead, Westbury, and Roslyn — in order.)

7. NEWPORT. Having finally reached Newport, be very careful about the pace. Begin cautiously with Bellevue Avenue and the casino. Gradually, however, you may hit up the pace and try the golf

club, Bailey's Beach, and, finally, you may dash past the judge's stand and weigh in at Ochre Point.

※

AT Newport the hostess usually retires at about 1.30. This should be the signal for all the bachelors, diplomats, and foreigners who are stopping with her, to ask the butler for carriages and motors to convey them to Canfield's (a fashionable roulette and chicken-salad parlor).

※

A BACHELOR stopping with friends in Newport should never lunch or dine in their house. It is more jaunty to dine out. If they are truly considerate, they will supply him with red morocco " in-and-out " signs which he can manipulate, in accordance with his engagements, in the entrance hall.

After a week or so, if he has not yet seen his host or hostess and is preparing to leave Newport, it is sometimes thoughtful and kind to send a card up to their rooms by a servant, thanking them for their hospitality.

GENERAL RULES

GENERAL RULES

WEDDING receptions are usually held in small private houses holding anywhere from one hundred to two hundred guests. It is customary to invite sixteen hundred people, six hundred of whom arrive and three hundred of whom usually remain wedged for hours upon the stairs in a bewildering sea of picture hats, lobster salad, smilax, rice, and lady fingers.

※

AFTER a funeral it is customary for the family to supply a few extra carriages in which the pallbearers and mourners go to the burial ground. After this ceremony the bachelor, who has availed himself of one of the vehicles, may, with propriety, ask the driver to take him to his rooms; but it is a gross breach of good form to keep the carriage on (at the family's expense) for calling, going to the play, or driving to Belmont Park for the races.

IN thanking friends for wedding presents, it is well to remember that nearly all of them will have to be exchanged. Lay your plans accordingly. Do not thank anybody until you have bunched the duplicates.

Let us assume, for instance, that the seventeen traveling clocks, forty-eight candlesticks, eleven porcelain parasol handles, fifty-one cut-glass salad bowls, thirteen fans, and eighty-four silver teapots have all been gathered together in convenient groups. At this point the bride-to-be may dictate an appropriate "teapot" letter to her secretary. This note will do for *all* the teapots. The following is a graceful example of such an epistle:

My dear —— ——:

The teapot is *too* ravishing. What an *angel* you are! I simply *adore* it. Oddly enough, it was the *very* thing I had longed and *prayed* for.
Yours ever,
Blanche.

P. S. — Where did you say you bought it?

When a lady calls you up on the telephone, and seems disposed to run on forever, simply hang up the receiver and go on with your cigar. If she calls up again to complete the conversation, tell your servant to say that you were disgusted with the way the central girl cut you off and have gone to the telephone company to lodge a complaint.

BE careful to remember that the lady always bows first. On some occasions it is difficult to determine whether the fast-approaching queen of fashion is going to bow or not. Should you be walking down the avenue with another man, proceed as follows: Look at her and exclaim gladly: " Why, how do you do—" Should she freeze, or cut you, you have but to turn to your friend and complete your remark by adding—" that little trick you showed me yesterday?"

Thus, it may appear to him that your remark was meant to be a continuous one, having to do with some feat of legerdemain, and he will fail to notice the snub which has been so cruelly inflicted upon you.

PROPOSALS by women, while permissible, are not customary, and, although they are yearly becoming more and more popular, are still regarded as an innovation. If the proposal is rejected, good taste and kindly consideration demand that the gentleman should keep it more or less of a secret.

It is, of course, not always easy for a gentleman to know when he has been definitely proposed to. Women's ways are sometimes devious and obscure. Roughly speaking, it is a proposal, or its equivalent, when a lady throws her head upon his breast and bursts into a passionate flood of tears.

T HE duties of a valet in a country house are as follows:

(1) Talking and snickering to the housemaids in the hallways.

(2) Purloining little keepsakes from the portmanteaus of the visitors.

MANNERS *for the* METROPOLIS

(3) Bouncing into the bachelors' rooms one hour before they wish to be wakened, in order to build fires, close bureau drawers, misinform them about the weather, and take away dress coats and trousers.

(4) Laying out clothes in the morning. In doing this they usually exhibit a highly trained color sense, selecting as the smartest combination of apparel a blue shirt, brown socks, lilac handkerchief, green tie, and a yellow waistcoat.

(5) Standing in a conspicuous position in the main hallway on Monday morning, which is always the period of largess and plenty.

(6) Wrapping up muddy boots in black evening trousers.

(7) Perhaps, however, their most blissful moment is when, knowing that you have one more evening before you, they take your only remaining white shirt, fold it into a sausage-shaped roll, and hurl it into the soiled-linen basket.

MANNERS *for the* METROPOLIS

A MOVEMENT is on foot in polite society to revise the barbarous wedding anniversaries as at present regulated, as modern marriages seldom last long enough to celebrate them. It is proposed, therefore, to call the first anniversary the tin, the second the silver, the third the gold, as marriages in society are only contracted, on one side or the other, for the attainment of these several commodities.

WHEN ladies are introduced to one another, they should remain rigid and calm and evince no interest in the proceeding. Their necks should be stiff and their heads thrown back—like cobras about to strike.

AT a wedding it is not customary for the best man to kiss the bride. Should the occasion seem, however, to call for such an act, he should be careful only to deliver a "Sweeper." A "Dweller" may alone be administered by the groom.

※

A BACHELOR should supply the telephone girl at his office with a list of ladies to whom he is always "out." On a select list he will write the names of five or six ladies who entertain delightfully and to whom he is always "in."

※

IN introducing two people show no sign of emotion whatever. Merely look from one to the other in a vague, listless sort of way, and murmur their names very swiftly and very faintly. It is, of course, bad form to introduce at all, but, if put to it, proceed as above.

At Christmas time a married man should make certain to tip the telephone boy at his club. If the lad is clever enough to recognize the voice of the member's wife, at the other end of the telephone, he should receive ten dollars. If he recognizes *other* female voices as well, he should receive twenty.

※

A CHIVALROUS husband should always try, by kindly acts and little courtesies, to ingratiate himself in his wife's affections. It is, for instance, selfish of him to return from his office to his home before dressing time.

He should remember that the hours between 4.15 and 7.15 are *her* hours. In this brief space she will probably wish to pour tea, entertain male visitors, play bridge, buy jewelry, take a nap, or have her hair "marcelled," and the husband should always consider her feelings during this trying part of the day. He may solace himself by remembering that the sitting rooms of other ladies are always open to him during these hours. If not, he can always go to the steam room at a Turkish bath, or drop in at the " Plaza " and hear the *nouveaux riches* drink tea.

IN motoring, avoid running over hens, dogs, and Italian children. They are almost certain to stick up the wheels.

CHURCH-GOING is no longer considered fashionable. If a lady finds that she *must* attend church, it is a wise precaution to take a little child with her. This will not only make a good impression but will give her an excellent excuse for leaving before the sermon.

※

WHEN you are northbound and a lady bows to you from a southbound brougham, do not trouble to lift your hat. Merely raise your arm halfway to your head, as the vehicle will have passed in a moment and your failure to bow is certain to remain unnoticed.

※

ALWAYS be half an hour late for everything. Nothing is so tedious as waiting.

THE END

onversation